Needs and Wants

Doug Bradley

INFOMAX COMMON CORE READERS

Rosen Classroom™

New York

Published in 2013 by The Rosen Publishing Group, Inc.
29 East 21st Street, New York, NY 10010

Book Design: Michael Harmon

Photo Credits: Cover (red peppers, lemons, cucumbers) Viktar Malyshchyts/Shutterstock.com; cover, p. 14 (doctor) Stephen Coburn/Shutterstock.com; cover, p. 5 (necklace) Africa Studio/Shutterstock.com; cover, p. 10 (skateboard kids) Dmitriy Shironosov/Shutterstock.com; cover, p. 9 (soccer team) © iStockphoto.com/CEFutcher; cover, p. 8 (milkshake kids) Ryan McVay/Stone/Getty Images; cover, p. 6 (lollipops) Junial Enterprises/Shutterstock.com; cover, p. 7 (girls eating salad) © iStockphoto.com/ktaylorg; cover, p. 12 (swimmers) Golden Pixels/Shutterstock.com; cover, p. 4 (chocolate) Shebeko/Shutterstock.com; cover, p. 13 (family with house) Andy Dean Photography/Shutterstock.com; cover, p. 5 (plaid shirt) Karkas/Shutterstock.com; cover, p. 11 (winter kids) Eric Lemon/Shutterstock.com; cover, p. 14 (teacher) Dmitriy Shironosov/Shutterstock.com; p. 4 (apple) atoss/ Shutterstock.com.

ISBN: 978-1-4488-8947-1
6-pack ISBN: 978-1-4488-8948-8

Manufactured in the United States of America

CPSIA Compliance Information: Batch #WS12RC: For further information contact Rosen Publishing, New York, New York at 1-800-237-9932.

Word Count: 104

Contents

What are needs?

What are wants?

We cannot live without the things we need.

We can live without the things we want.

We want to eat candy.

Candy is fun to eat.

We need to eat healthy foods.

Healthy foods are good for us.

We want to drink milkshakes.

Milkshakes are fun to drink.

We need to drink water.

Water is good for us.

We want new skateboards.

Skateboards are fun.

We need clothes.

Clothes keep us warm.

We want a pool.

Pools are fun.

We need a home.

A home will keep us safe.

Can you think of other things
that we need?

Needs and Wants

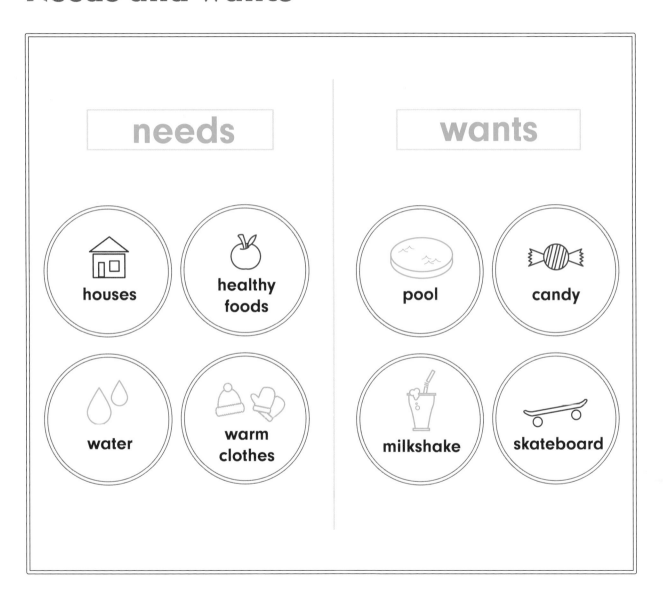

needs
- houses
- healthy foods
- water
- warm clothes

wants
- pool
- candy
- milkshake
- skateboard

Words to Know

clothes

milkshake

pool

skateboard

Index